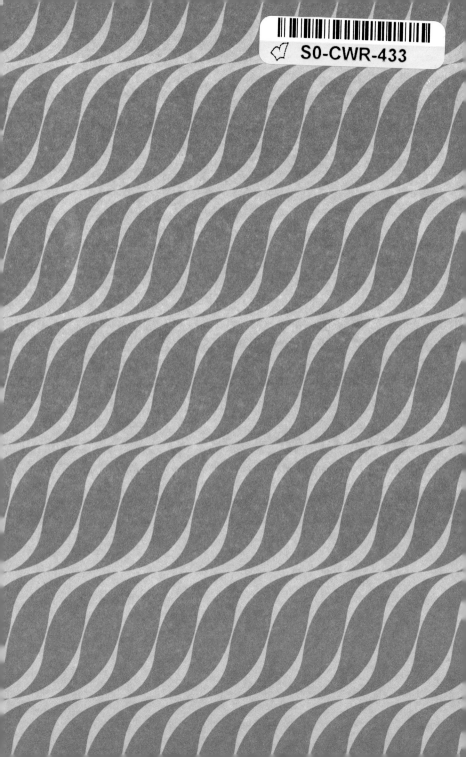

COOKIES

Consultant Editor:
Valerie Ferguson

southwater

Contents

Introduction

There is something very comforting about cookies and biscuits and the way they fill a gap as nothing else does, whether with a cup of coffee for a quick mid-morning break, an after-school snack to keep the kids going until supper time or with cheese after dinner. They are easy to make and take very little time, so you can always have a good supply in the cupboard – or even in the freezer for when unexpected guests drop in. As with so much home cooking, cookies and biscuits from your own kitchen are much tastier than shop-bought ones and won't include artificial flavours and preservatives. They will cost a lot less too, and, perhaps just as importantly, making them is fun.

This book is packed with recipes for both sweet and savoury biscuits, using a vast range of ingredients from cheese to herbs and spices, and from fruit and nuts to chocolate. There is something for everyone – buttery shortcake for traditionalists, Chocolate Chip Cookies for children, rich fudgy bars for chocoholics and spicy crackers for the less sweet-toothed. There is even a selection of delicious low-fat recipes. Suitable for so many occasions, home-made cookies and biscuits are a really tasty treat.

Ingredients

Many types of biscuits can be made from store cupboard items, but some will require fresh ingredients.

Dairy Products & Substitutes

Butter

Butter makes the richest biscuits with the lightest texture. Use unsalted or lightly salted butter for sweet biscuits. Margarine is also good, but tends to make more brittle biscuits. Low-fat spreads are suitable for many recipes, but do lack richness. They are useful for healthy eating and for those on a low-fat diet.

Milk

Milk, yogurt, soured cream, cream and crème fraîche can all be used to bind the dough, giving slightly different flavours and textures.

Some biscuits are filled or sandwiched together with cream. In such cases, use whipping or double cream. Soft cheeses can also be used for fillings. Grated cheese is a wonderful flavouring for savoury biscuits. For best results, use hard or semi-hard cheeses, such as Parmesan or Cheddar. Eggs are also commonly used for binding the dough and, for best results, use free-range, organic eggs.

Parmesan Cheese

Eggs

Flour

Plain flour is the most commonly used. For best results, choose organic stone-ground flour. Wholemeal flour is well-suited to savoury biscuits, while soft flour, sometimes called sponge flour may be used on its own or mixed with plain flour for sweet cookies.

Fruit

Dried Apricots

Dried fruit is featured in many recipes and includes not only traditional sultanas and raisins, but also more unusual varieties, such as apricots. The natural sugars add sweetness and moistness. Glacé cherries and candied fruit and peel may be used for decoration and also form an integral part of some biscuits, such as florentines.

Sultanas

Glacé Cherries

Apart from very firm berries, fresh fruit is rarely used other than for decoration, as it tends to make biscuits soggy. Fruit juices, however, can supply the flavour and natural sweetness of fresh fruit, so they are useful for binding the dough and flavouring fillings. Pear and apple spread, a concentrated fruit juice, is also excellent for binding and providing sweetness and flavour.

Flavourings

Unsweetened cocoa powder, plain, milk or white chocolate and chocolate chips are widely used, both for flavouring and decoration. Grated citrus rind and vanilla and almond essences feature in many recipes. Coffee, often in the form of instant powder, is a popular flavouring. Brandy, whisky and liqueurs add warm and sophisticated flavours to cookies.

Plain Chocolate

White Chocolate

Vanilla Essence

Grains

Rolled oats and oatmeal feature in many traditional recipes. Cornmeal makes lovely golden biscuits. Muesli and breakfast cereals are also useful.

Oats

Herbs & Spices

Chopped fresh herbs may be used to add interest, particularly to savoury biscuits. Common spices for sweet biscuits are ground cinnamon, nutmeg and ginger. Savoury biscuits may also include spices or curry powder.

Ground Cinnamon

Nuts & Seeds

Traditional favourites are coconut, usually desiccated, walnuts, hazelnuts, pecan nuts, almonds and pine nuts. Seeds, such as sesame, sunflower and poppy, may be added to sweet or savoury biscuits. They give additional texture, flavour and nutrients.

Hazelnuts

Sweeteners

Caster sugar is easily incorporated into dough, although granulated is sometimes suggested. Unrefined sugars, such as dark muscovado, have more flavour, add colour and contain some minerals. Honey has a strong flavour and is sweeter than sugar, so you can use less of it than the equivalent of sugar. Molasses and black treacle have a smoky flavour and slightly bitter taste. They go well with other strong flavours, such as ginger. Malt extract is also distinctive and is a good choice for softer bakes, as it adds moistness. Golden, corn and maple syrup are very sweet with a more subtle flavour. Always use pure maple syrup for the best flavour. Syrup is essential for some very light biscuits, such as crisp brandy snaps.

Muscovado Sugar

Honey

Techniques

Stencilling

Use stencils to liven up biscuits in a simple and fun way.

1 Cut a small design or initial out of card and place it over a biscuit. Dust with icing sugar or cocoa before carefully removing the card.

Grinding Nuts

Using a nut mill or a clean coffee grinder, grind a small batch of nuts at a time to ensure an even texture. As soon as the nuts have a fine texture, stop grinding; if overworked, they will turn to paste. Alternatively, use a food processor. To avoid overworking the nuts add some of the sugar or flour needed in the recipe.

Roasting Nuts

Roasting nuts brings out their flavour and makes them crunchier.

1 To oven-roast or grill nuts: spread the nuts on a baking sheet. Roast in a 180°C/350°F/Gas 4 oven or under a moderate grill, until golden brown and smelling nutty. Stir the nuts occasionally to brown evenly.

2 To dry-roast nuts: put the nuts in a frying pan, with no fat. Roast over moderate heat until golden brown. Stir constantly and watch carefully: nuts can scorch easily.

COOK'S TIP: Set the timer for 3-4 minutes when oven-roasting nuts.

Melting Chocolate

There are basically three simple ways to melt chocolate:

Melting Over Hot Water

1 Fill a saucepan about a quarter full with water. Place a heatproof bowl on top. The water should not touch the bowl. Bring the water to simmering point, then lower the heat.

2 Break the chocolate into squares and place in the bowl. Leave to melt completely, without stirring. Keep the water at a very low simmer.

COOK'S TIP: The melted chocolate should be only just warm and never allowed to boil. Also, ensure that no water gets into the bowl.

Melting in the Microwave

1 Break the chocolate into squares and place it in a microwave-safe bowl. Heat in the microwave until just softened, checking frequently.

Approximate times for melting in a 650–700 watt microwave oven:
115 g/4 oz plain or milk chocolate
  2 minutes on High (100% power)
115 g/4 oz white chocolate
  2 minutes on Medium (50% power)

Direct Heat Method

1 This is only suitable where the chocolate is melted in plenty of liquid. Add the broken chocolate to the liquid in the pan, then heat gently, stirring occasionally, until the chocolate has melted and the mixture is smooth.

Oatcakes

These are very simple to make and are an excellent addition to the after-dinner cheese board.

Makes 24

INGREDIENTS
225 g/8 oz/2 cups medium oatmeal,
   plus extra for dusting
75 g/3 oz/¾ cup plain flour
1.5 ml/¼ tsp bicarbonate of soda
5 ml/1 tsp salt
25 g/1 oz/2 tbsp hard white vegetable fat
25 g/1 oz/2 tbsp butter

1 Preheat the oven to 220°C/425°F/ Gas 7. Place the oatmeal, flour, bicarbonate of soda and salt in a large bowl. Melt the vegetable fat and butter together in a pan over a low heat.

2 Add the melted fat and enough boiling water to the bowl to make a soft dough. Turn out on to a surface scattered with a little oatmeal. Roll out the dough thinly and cut it into circles. Bake the oatcakes on ungreased baking trays for 15 minutes, until crisp.

Cheddar Pennies

These delicious little snacks look innocent, but are full of flavour with just a hint of chilli. They are perfect to serve with drinks.

Makes 20

INGREDIENTS

50 g/2 oz/¼ cup butter, at room temperature, plus extra for greasing
115 g/4 oz/1 cup grated Cheddar cheese
40 g/1½ oz/⅓ cup plain flour, plus extra for dusting
pinch of chilli powder
salt

1 With an electric mixer, cream the butter until soft. Stir in the cheese, flour, chilli and a pinch of salt. Gather to form a dough.

2 Transfer to a floured surface. Shape into a cylinder about 3 cm/1¼ in in diameter. Wrap in greaseproof paper and chill in the fridge for 1–2 hours.

3 Preheat the oven to 180°C/350°F/ Gas 4. Grease one or two baking sheets. Slice the dough into 5 mm/¼ in thick rounds and place on the prepared baking sheets. Bake the biscuits for about 15 minutes, or until golden. Transfer to a wire rack to cool.

VARIATION: Try Edam, Gruyère or double Gloucester in these biscuits.

Rosemary Biscuits

These biscuits are flavoured with rosemary and garnished with the flowers.
They are delicious either on their own or with a mild-flavoured cheese.

Makes 25

INGREDIENTS
225 g/8 oz/2 cups plain flour, plus extra
    for dusting
2.5 ml/½ tsp baking powder
2.5 ml/½ tsp curry powder
75 g/3 oz/6 tbsp butter, diced
30 ml/2 tbsp finely chopped young
    rosemary leaves
1 egg yolk
30–45 ml/2–3 tbsp water
milk, to glaze
salt
30 ml/2 tbsp cream cheese
rosemary flowers

1 Put the flour, baking powder, curry powder and a pinch of salt in a bowl.

2 Rub the butter into the flour until the mixture resembles fine breadcrumbs. Add the rosemary, egg yolk and sufficient water to mix to a firm dough. Chill for 30 minutes.

3 Preheat the oven to 180°C/350°F/ Gas 4. Roll the dough thinly on a lightly floured surface and cut out rounds using a 5 cm/2 in fluted cutter.

4 Transfer to a large baking sheet and prick with a fork. Brush with milk to glaze and bake for 10 minutes, or until pale golden. Cool on a wire rack.

5 Spread a little cream cheese on to each biscuit and secure some rosemary flowers on top.

Parmesan Thins

These melt-in-the-mouth biscuits are very moreish, so make plenty. Don't just keep them for parties – they make a great snack at any time of the day.

Makes 16–20

INGREDIENTS
50 g/2 oz/½ cup plain flour
40 g/1½ oz/3 tbsp butter, softened
1 egg yolk
40 g/1½ oz/½ cup freshly grated
    Parmesan cheese
pinch of dry mustard
salt

1 Rub together the flour and the butter in a bowl, then work in the egg yolk, cheese, mustard and a pinch of salt. Mix to bring the dough together into a ball. Shape into a log, then wrap in foil or clear film and chill in the fridge for at least 10 minutes.

2 Preheat the oven to 200°C/400°F/ Gas 6. Cut the dough log into very thin slices, about 3–5 mm/⅛–¼ in, and arrange on a baking sheet. Flatten with a fork to give a pretty ridged pattern.

3 Bake for 10 minutes, or until crisp but not changing colour. Transfer to a wire rack to cool.

Spiced Cocktail Biscuits

These savoury biscuits are ideal for serving with pre-dinner drinks. Each type of seed contributes to the flavour.

Makes 20–30

INGREDIENTS
115 g/4 oz/½ cup butter, plus extra
   for greasing
150 g/5 oz/1¼ cups plain flour, plus
   extra for dusting
10 ml/2 tsp curry powder
75 g/3 oz/¾ cup grated
   Cheddar cheese
10 ml/2 tsp poppy seeds
5 ml/1 tsp black onion seeds
1 egg yolk
cumin seeds, to garnish

1 Grease two baking sheets. Sift the flour and curry powder into a bowl.

2 Rub in the butter until the mixture resembles breadcrumbs, then stir in the cheese, poppy seeds and black onion seeds. Stir in the egg yolk and mix to a firm dough. Wrap the dough in clear film and chill in the fridge for 30 minutes.

3 Roll out the dough on a floured surface to a thickness of about 3 mm/⅛ in. Cut into shapes with a biscuit cutter. Arrange on the prepared baking sheets and sprinkle with cumin seeds. Chill for 15 minutes.

4 Preheat the oven to 190°C/375°F/ Gas 5. Bake the biscuits for about 20 minutes, until crisp and golden. Serve warm or cold.

Curry Crackers

These spicy, crisp little biscuits are very low in fat and are ideal for serving with drinks or dips.

Makes 12

INGREDIENTS

50 g/2 oz/½ cup plain flour, plus extra
    for dusting
1.5 ml/¼ tsp salt
5 ml/1 tsp curry powder
1.5 ml/¼ tsp chilli powder
15 ml/1 tbsp chopped fresh coriander
30 ml/2 tbsp water

1 Preheat the oven to 180°C/350°F/ Gas 4. Sift the flour and salt into a mixing bowl, then add the curry powder and chilli powder. Make a well in the centre and add the coriander and water. Gradually incorporate the flour and mix to a firm dough.

2 Turn on to a lightly floured surface, knead until smooth, then leave to rest for 5 minutes.

3 Cut the dough into 12 pieces and knead into small balls. Roll each ball out very thinly to a 10 cm/4 in round.

4 Arrange the rounds on two ungreased baking sheets, then bake for 15 minutes, turning over once during cooking. Transfer to a wire rack to cool completely.

VARIATIONS: Omit the curry and chilli powders and add 15 ml/1 tbsp caraway, fennel or mustard seeds.

Vanilla Crescents

These attractive little almond and vanilla-flavoured biscuits are absolutely irresistible.

Makes 36

INGREDIENTS
175 g/6 oz/1 cup unblanched almonds
115 g/4 oz/1 cup plain flour
2.5 ml/½ tsp salt
225 g/8 oz/1 cup butter, at room temperature, plus extra for greasing
90 g/3½ oz/½ cup sugar
5 ml/1 tsp vanilla essence
icing sugar, for dusting

1 Put the almonds and a few tablespoons of the flour in a food processor or blender, and process.

2 Sift the remaining flour with the salt. Set aside. With an electric mixer, cream the butter and sugar together in a bowl until light and fluffy.

3 Add the almonds, vanilla essence and the flour mixture. Stir to mix well. Gather the dough into a ball, wrap in greaseproof paper and chill in the fridge for at least 30 minutes.

4 Preheat the oven to 160°C/325°F/ Gas 3. Lightly grease two baking sheets. Break off walnut-size pieces of dough and roll into small cylinders about 1 cm/½ in diameter. Bend into small crescents and place on the prepared baking sheets.

5 Bake for about 20 minutes, until dry but not brown. Transfer to a rack to cool slightly. Set the rack over a baking sheet and dust with an even layer of icing sugar.

COOK'S TIPS: Chilling the biscuit dough makes it firmer and therefore easier to shape.
   Bake biscuits at or just above the centre of the oven. If you are using two baking sheets, place one above the other and swap them over halfway through the cooking time, so that they brown evenly.

Gingersnaps

Crisp and crunchy, gingersnaps are firm favourites with all the family.

Makes 60

INGREDIENTS
115 g/4 oz/½ cup butter, at room
    temperature, plus extra for greasing
275 g/10 oz/2½ cups plain flour
5 ml/1 tsp bicarbonate of soda
7.5 ml/1½ tsp ground ginger
1.5 ml/¼ tsp ground cinnamon
1.5 ml/¼ tsp ground cloves
300 g/11 oz/generous 1½ cups sugar
1 egg, lightly beaten
60 ml/4 tbsp molasses or black treacle
5 ml/1 tsp lemon juice

1 Preheat the oven to 180°C/350°F/
Gas 4. Grease three or four baking
sheets. Sift the flour, bicarbonate of
soda, ginger, cinnamon and cloves into
a bowl. Set aside.

2 With an electric mixer, cream the
butter and 200 g/7 oz/1 cup of the
sugar together. Stir in the egg, molasses
or treacle and lemon juice. Add the
flour mixture and mix thoroughly with
a wooden spoon to make a soft dough.

3 Shape into 2 cm/¾ in balls. Roll
the balls in the remaining sugar and
place 5 cm/2 in apart on the baking
sheets. Bake for 12 minutes, or until
just firm.

Right: Gingersnaps (top); Cowboy Bakes

Cowboy Bakes

There'll be no need to corral the kids at teatime for these tasty treats.

Makes 60

INGREDIENTS
115 g/4 oz/½ cup butter, plus extra
    for greasing
115 g/4 oz/1 cup plain flour
2.5 ml/½ tsp bicarbonate of soda
1.5 ml/¼ tsp baking powder
1.5 ml/¼ tsp salt
90 g/3½ oz/½ cup granulated sugar
115 g/4 oz/½ cup brown sugar
1 egg
2.5 ml/½ tsp vanilla essence
90 g/3½ oz/1 cup rolled oats
175 g/6 oz/1 cup milk chocolate chips

1 Preheat the oven to 160°C/325°F/
Gas 3. Grease three or four baking
sheets. Sift the flour, bicarbonate of
soda, baking powder and salt into a
mixing bowl. Set aside.

2 With an electric mixer, cream the
butter and sugars together. Add the egg
and vanilla and beat until light and
fluffy. Add the flour mixture and beat
on low speed until blended. Stir in the
oats and chocolate, mixing well. The
dough should be crumbly.

3 Drop heaped teaspoons on to the
baking sheets, about 2.5 cm/1 in apart.
Bake for 15 minutes, or until just firm
around the edge. Transfer to a wire
rack to cool.

Macaroons

If you have only ever eaten ready-made macaroons, this recipe will be a wonderful revelation for your taste buds.

Makes about 30

INGREDIENTS
sunflower oil for greasing
2 egg yolks
1 egg white
200 g/7 oz/1¾ cups icing sugar, plus extra
    for dusting
10 ml/2 tsp baking powder
grated rind of ½ lemon
a few drops of vanilla essence
about 350 g/12 oz/3 cups ground almonds

1 Preheat the oven to 180°C/350°F/ Gas 4. Grease a baking sheet with sunflower oil. Beat together the egg yolks and egg white with the icing sugar in a bowl.

2 Add the baking powder, grated lemon rind and vanilla essence, with enough of the ground almonds to make a stiff paste.

3 Knead the mixture together with your hands. Oil your hands with sunflower oil. Take walnut-size pieces of paste and roll into small balls. Flatten on a board dusted with icing sugar and then place on the prepared baking sheet about 4 cm/1½ in apart.

4 Bake for 15 minutes, until golden. Transfer to a wire rack to cool.

Hazelnut Bites

Serve these sweet Italian nut cookies as petits fours with after-dinner coffee as well as at tea time.

Makes about 26

INGREDIENTS
115 g/4 oz/½ cup butter, softened
75 g/3 oz/¾ cup icing sugar, sifted
115 g/4 oz/1 cup plain flour
75 g/3 oz/¾ cup ground hazelnuts
1 egg yolk

FOR THE DECORATION
blanched whole hazelnuts
icing sugar

1 Preheat the oven to 180°C/350°F/Gas 4. Line baking sheets with non-stick baking paper. Cream the butter and sugar together with an electric mixer until light and fluffy.

2 Beat in the flour, ground hazelnuts and egg yolk until evenly mixed.

3 Take a teaspoonful of the mixture at a time and shape it into a round with your fingers. Place the rounds well apart on the baking paper and press a whole hazelnut into the centre of each one.

4 Bake the biscuits, one tray at a time, for about 10 minutes, or until golden brown; the biscuits will still be soft at the end of the baking time and will harden as they cool.

5 Transfer to a wire rack and sift over icing sugar to cover. Leave to cool.

21

Lavender Heart Cookies

Serve these fragrant cookies on any romantic anniversary.

Makes 16–18

INGREDIENTS
115 g/4 oz/½ cup unsalted butter
90 ml/6 tbsp caster sugar
175 g/6 oz/1½ cups plain flour, plus extra
    for dusting
30 ml/2 tbsp fresh lavender florets
    or 15 ml/1 tbsp dried culinary lavender,
    roughly chopped

1 Cream the butter and 60 ml/4 tbsp of sugar together until fluffy. Stir in the flour and lavender and bring the mixture together in a soft ball. Cover and chill in the fridge for 15 minutes.

2 Preheat the oven to 200°C/400°F/ Gas 6. Roll out the dough on a lightly floured surface and stamp out about 18 cookies, using a 5 cm/2 in heart-shaped cutter. Place on a heavy baking sheet and bake for about 10 minutes, or until golden.

3 Leave the cookies standing for 5 minutes, then transfer them carefully to a wire rack to cool.

COOK'S TIP: These cookies would make an unusual gift, contained in an airtight jar decorated with ribbon.

Chocolate Crackle-tops

Makes about 38 cookies

INGREDIENTS
200 g/7 oz bittersweet or semi-sweet
    chocolate, chopped
90 g/3½ oz/7 tbsp unsalted butter, plus extra
    for greasing
115 g/4 oz/⅔ cup caster sugar
3 eggs
5 ml/1 tsp vanilla essence
215 g/7½ oz/scant 2 cups plain flour
25 g/1 oz/¼ cup unsweetened cocoa
2.5 ml/½ tsp baking powder
pinch of salt
175 g/6 oz/1½ cups icing sugar

1 Heat the chocolate and butter in a medium saucepan over low heat until smooth, stirring frequently. Remove from heat. Add the sugar, stirring for 2–3 minutes, until it dissolves. Add the eggs, one at a time, beating well after each addition. Stir in the vanilla.

2 Sift the flour, cocoa, baking powder and salt into a bowl. Gradually stir into the chocolate mixture until blended. Cover and chill for at least 1 hour.

3 Preheat the oven to 160°C/325°F/ Gas 3. Grease two baking sheets. Place the icing sugar in a small bowl. Take teaspoonfuls of dough and roll into 4 cm/1½ in balls.

4 Drop the balls, one at a time, into the icing sugar and roll until heavily coated. Remove with a slotted spoon and tap against the side of the bowl to remove any excess sugar. Place on baking sheets 4 cm/1½ in apart.

5 Bake the cookies for 10–15 minutes, or until slightly firm when touched. Leave on the baking sheet for 2–3 minutes to set then cool on a wire rack.

Brittany Butter Biscuits

These delicious, melt-in-the-mouth biscuits from northern France are similar to shortbread, but richer.

Makes 18–20

INGREDIENTS

200 g/7 oz/scant 1 cup lightly salted butter, at room temperature, diced, plus extra for greasing
6 egg yolks, lightly beaten
15 ml/1 tbsp milk
250 g/9 oz/generous 2 cups plain flour
175 g/6 oz/scant 1 cup caster sugar

1 Preheat the oven to 180°C/350°F/ Gas 4. Lightly grease a large, heavy baking sheet. Mix 15 ml/1 tbsp of the egg yolks with the milk to make a glaze and set aside.

2 Sift the flour into a large bowl and make a well in the centre. Add the sugar and butter, then the remaining egg yolks. Using your fingertips, work the mixture together until smooth and creamy.

3 Gradually incorporate the flour from the edge of the well, to form a smooth, slightly sticky dough.

4 Using floured hands, pat out the dough to about a 5 mm/¼ in thickness and cut out rounds using a 7.5 cm/ 3 in cutter. Transfer to the baking sheet, brush with a little glaze, then using the back of a knife, score with lines to create a lattice pattern.

5 Bake the biscuits for 12–15 minutes, or until golden. Cool on the baking sheet on a wire rack for 15 minutes, then transfer the biscuits to the rack to cool completely.

Muesli Biscuits

Best made with good-quality muesli.

Makes 18

INGREDIENTS
115 g/4 oz/½ cup butter, at room
    temperature, plus extra for greasing
115 g/4 oz/½ cup light brown sugar
75 ml/5 tbsp crunchy peanut butter
1 egg
50 g/2 oz/½ cup plain flour
2.5 ml/½ tsp baking powder
2.5 ml/½ tsp cinnamon
pinch of salt
225 g/8 oz/2 cups muesli
40 g/1½ oz/⅓ cup raisins
50 g/2 oz/½ cup walnuts, chopped

1 Preheat the oven to 180°C/350°F/
Gas 4. Grease a baking sheet. With an
electric mixer, cream the butter and
sugar until light and fluffy. Beat in the
peanut butter, then beat in the egg.

2 Sift the flour, baking powder,
cinnamon and salt over the peanut
butter mixture and stir. Stir in the
muesli, raisins and walnuts.

3 Drop rounded tablespoonfuls of
the batter on to the prepared baking
sheet about 5 cm/2 in apart. Press
gently with the back of a spoon to
spread each mound into a circle.
Bake for 15 minutes, or until lightly
coloured. Cool on a wire rack.

Oatmeal Cereal Cookies

Satisfying and crunchy snacks.

Makes 14

INGREDIENTS
175 g/6 oz/¾ cup butter, at room
    temperature, plus extra for greasing
150 g/5 oz/¾ cup sugar
1 egg yolk
175 g/6 oz/1½ cups plain flour, plus extra
    for dusting
5 ml/1 tsp bicarbonate of soda
2.5 ml/½ tsp salt
50 g/2 oz/scant ½ cup rolled oats
50 g/2 oz/scant ½ cup crunchy
    granola-type cereal

1 With an electric mixer, cream the
butter and sugar together until light
and fluffy. Mix in the egg yolk. Sift
over the flour, bicarbonate of soda and
salt, then stir into the butter mixture.
Add the oats and cereal and stir to
blend. Chill for at least 20 minutes.

2 Preheat the oven to 190°C/375°F/
Gas 5. Grease a baking sheet. Roll the
dough into balls. Place them on the
baking sheet and flatten with the
bottom of a floured glass.

3 Bake for 10–12 minutes, or until
golden. Transfer to a wire rack to cool.

Right: Muesli Biscuits (top);
Oatmeal Cereal Cookies

Sultana Biscuits

Makes about 48

INGREDIENTS
75 g/3 oz/½ cup sultanas
225 g/8 oz/1 cup butter, plus extra
    for greasing
115 g/4 oz/1 cup finely ground
    yellow cornmeal
175 g/6 oz/1½ cups plain flour
7.5 ml/1½ tsp baking powder
2.5 ml/½ tsp salt
225 g/8 oz/generous 1 cup
    granulated sugar
2 eggs
15 ml/1 tbsp Marsala or 5 ml/1 tsp
    vanilla essence

1 Soak the sultanas in a small bowl
of warm water for 15 minutes. Drain.
Preheat the oven to 180°C/350°F/
Gas 4. Grease two baking sheets.

2 Sift the cornmeal, flour, baking
powder and salt into a bowl. Cream
the butter and sugar together until
light and fluffy. Beat in the eggs, one at
a time. Beat in the Marsala or vanilla
essence. Add the dry ingredients to the
batter, beating until well blended. Stir
in the sultanas.

3 Drop heaped teaspoons of batter
on to the baking sheets in rows about
5 cm/2 in apart. Bake for 7–8 minutes,
or until golden brown at the edges.
Transfer to a wire rack to cool.

Right: Sultana Biscuits (top); Amaretti

Amaretti

Makes about 36

INGREDIENTS
200 g/7 oz/1¼ cups almonds
225 g/8 oz/generous 1 cup caster sugar
2 egg whites
2.5 ml/½ tsp almond essence
flour, for dusting
icing sugar, for dusting

1 Preheat the oven to 160°C/325°F/
Gas 3. Drop the almonds into a pan of
boiling water for 1–2 minutes. Drain
and rub in a cloth to remove the skins.
Spread out on a baking sheet and dry
out in the oven for 10–15 minutes
without browning. Remove from the
oven and allow to cool. Turn the oven
off. Finely grind the almonds with half
the sugar in a food processor.

2 Beat the egg whites until they form
soft peaks. Sprinkle half the remaining
sugar over them and continue beating.
Fold in the remaining sugar, the
almond essence and almonds.

3 Spoon the mixture into a pastry
bag with a smooth nozzle. Line a
baking sheet with non-stick baking
paper. Dust with flour. Pipe the
mixture in walnut-size rounds.
Sprinkle with icing sugar and set
aside for 2 hours. Preheat the oven
to 180°C/350°F/Gas 4.

4 Bake for 15 minutes, or until pale
gold. Cool on a wire rack.

Lepeshki

Soured cream is often used in Russian cooking; here, it is used instead of butter to make light biscuits.

Makes 24

INGREDIENTS
vegetable oil, for brushing
225 g/8 oz/2 cups self-raising flour, plus extra for dusting
90 g/3½ oz/½ cup caster sugar
1 egg, separated
120 ml/4 fl oz/½ cup soured cream
2.5 ml/½ tsp each vanilla and almond essence
15 ml/1 tbsp milk
50 g/2 oz/½ cup flaked almonds
salt

1 Preheat the oven to 200°C/400°F/Gas 6. Brush two baking sheets with oil. Sift the flour, sugar and a pinch of salt into a mixing bowl and make a well in the centre.

2 Reserve 10 ml/2 tsp of the egg white. Mix the remainder with the egg yolk, cream, vanilla and almond essences and milk. Add to the dry ingredients and mix to form a soft dough.

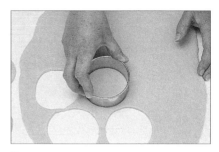

3 Roll out the dough on a lightly floured surface until about 8 mm/⅓ in thick, then stamp out rounds with a 7.5 cm/3 in cutter.

4 Transfer the rounds to the baking sheets, well spaced apart. Brush with the reserved egg white and sprinkle with the flaked almonds.

5 Bake for 10 minutes, or until a light golden brown. Transfer to a wire rack to cool.

VARIATION: Sesame seeds could be used in place of the almonds.

Chocolate Chip Cookies

Keep a supply of these favourite cookies stored in the freezer.

Makes 16

INGREDIENTS
75 g/3 oz/6 tbsp soft margarine, plus extra
    for greasing
50 g/2 oz/¼ cup light soft brown sugar
50 g/2 oz/¼ cup caster sugar
1 egg, beaten
few drops of vanilla essence
75 g/3 oz/¾ cup rice flour
75 g/3 oz/¾ cup cornmeal
5 ml/1 tsp baking powder
115 g/4 oz/⅔ cup plain chocolate chips, or a
    mixture of milk and white chocolate chips
salt

1 Preheat the oven to 190°C/375°F/ Gas 5. Lightly grease two baking sheets. Place the margarine and sugars in a bowl and cream together until light and fluffy.

2 Beat in the egg and vanilla essence. Fold in the rice flour, cornmeal, baking powder and a pinch of salt, then fold in the chocolate chips.

3 Place spoonfuls of the mixture on the baking sheets, spaced well apart. Bake for 10–15 minutes, until the cookies are lightly browned. Leave on the baking sheets for a few minutes, then cool on a wire rack.

Cherry Munchies

You'll find it hard to stop at just one of these munchies.

Makes 20

INGREDIENTS
2 egg whites
115 g/4 oz/1 cup icing
    sugar, sifted
115 g/4 oz/1 cup ground almonds
115 g/4 oz/generous 1 cup
    desiccated coconut
few drops of almond essence
75 g/3 oz/½ cup glacé cherries,
    finely chopped

1 Preheat the oven to 150°C/300°F/ Gas 2. Line two baking sheets with non-stick baking paper. Place the egg whites in a bowl and whisk until stiff.

2 Fold in the icing sugar, then fold in the ground almonds, coconut and almond essence to form a sticky dough. Fold in the chopped cherries.

3 Place heaped teaspoonfuls of the mixture on the prepared baking sheets. Bake for 25 minutes, or until pale golden. Cool on the baking sheets for a few minutes, then transfer to a wire rack until cold.

Right: Chocolate Chip Cookies (top); Cherry Munchies

Brandy Snaps

The combination of the crisp, light-as-air biscuit and rich, brandy-flavoured creamy filling is magical.

Makes 16

INGREDIENTS
50 g/2 oz/¼ cup butter, at room temperature,
    plus extra for greasing
130 g/4½ oz/⅔ cup sugar
20 ml/4 tsp golden syrup
40 g/1½ oz/⅓ cup plain flour
2.5 ml/½ tsp ground ginger

FOR THE FILLING
250 ml/8 fl oz/ 1 cup whipping cream
30 ml/2 tbsp brandy

1 With an electric mixer, cream together the butter and sugar until light and fluffy, then beat in the syrup. Sift over the flour and ginger and mix to a rough dough.

2 Transfer the dough to a work surface and knead until smooth. Cover and chill in the fridge for 30 minutes.

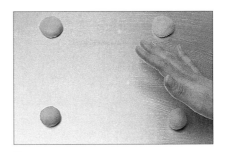

3 Preheat the oven to 190°C/375°F/Gas 5. Grease a baking sheet. Working in batches of four, form walnut-size balls of dough. Place far apart on the prepared sheet and flatten the balls slightly. Bake for about 10 minutes, or until golden and bubbling.

4 Remove from the oven and cool for a few moments. Working quickly, slide a palette knife under each one, turn over and wrap around the handle of a wooden spoon (have four spoons ready). If they firm up too quickly, reheat for a few seconds to soften. When firm, slide the snaps off and place on a rack to cool.

5 When all the brandy snaps are cool, prepare the filling. Whip the cream and brandy until soft peaks form. Fill a piping bag with the brandy cream. Pipe into each end of the brandy snaps just before serving.

Mini Florentines with Grand Marnier

Orange liqueur adds a luxury note to these ever-popular nut and dried fruit biscuits. Delicious on their own or with an iced dessert.

Makes about 24

INGREDIENTS

50 g/2 oz/¼ cup soft light brown sugar
15 ml/1 tbsp clear honey
15 ml/1 tbsp Grand Marnier
50 g/2 oz/¼ cup butter
40 g/1½ oz/⅓ cup plain flour
25 g/1 oz/¼ cup hazelnuts,
   roughly chopped
50 g/2 oz/½ cup flaked
   almonds, chopped
50 g/2 oz/¼ cup glacé
   cherries, chopped
115 g/4 oz dark chocolate, melted,
   for coating

2 Remove the pan from the heat and tip in the flour, hazelnuts, almonds and cherries. Stir well.

3 Spoon small heaps of the mixture on to the baking sheets. Bake for about 10 minutes, until golden brown. Leave the biscuits on the baking sheet until the edges begin to harden a little, then transfer to a wire rack to cool.

1 Preheat the oven to 180°C/350°F/ Gas 4. Line 3–4 baking sheets with non-stick baking paper. Combine the sugar, honey, Grand Marnier and butter in a small pan and melt over a low heat.

VARIATION: You could use melted white chocolate for the zigzag decoration, if you like.

4 Spread the melted chocolate over one side of each florentine, using a kitchen or palette knife. When it begins to set, drag a fork through to form wavy lines. Leave to set completely. Fill a piping bag with the remaining melted chocolate, snip off the end and pipe zigzag lines over the plain side of the florentines.

Almond Tile Biscuits

These biscuits are named after the French roof tiles they resemble. Making them is a little fiddly, so bake only four at a time until you get the knack.

Makes about 24

INGREDIENTS
40 g/1½ oz/3 tbsp unsalted butter, plus extra for greasing
65 g/2½ oz/½ cup whole blanched almonds, lightly toasted
65 g/2½ oz/⅓ cup caster sugar
2 egg whites
2.5 ml/½ tsp almond essence
35 g/1¼ oz/scant ⅓ cup plain flour, sifted
50 g/2 oz/½ cup flaked almonds

1 Preheat the oven to 200°C/400°F/Gas 6. Generously butter two heavy baking sheets.

2 Place the almonds and 30 ml/2 tbsp of the sugar in a food processor and pulse until finely ground, but not pasty.

3 With an electric mixer, beat the butter until creamy, then add the remaining caster sugar and beat for 12 minutes, until light and fluffy. Gradually beat in the egg whites, then beat in the almond essence. Sift the flour over the mixture and fold in, then fold in the ground almond mixture.

> COOK'S TIP: If the biscuits flatten or lose their crispness, reheat them on a baking sheet in a moderate oven, until completely flat, then reshape.

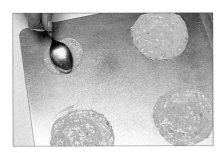

4 Drop tablespoons of mixture on to the baking sheets about 15 cm/6 in apart. With the back of a wet spoon, spread each mound into a paper-thin 7.5 cm/3 in round. (Don't worry if holes appear, they will fill in.) Sprinkle each round with a few flaked almonds.

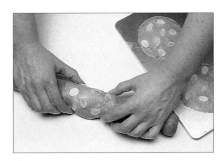

5 Bake the biscuits, one sheet at a time, for 5–6 minutes, or until the edges are golden and the centres still pale. Remove the baking sheet to a wire rack and, working quickly, use a thin palette knife to loosen the edges of one biscuit. Carefully place the biscuit over a rolling pin, then press down the sides of the biscuit to curve it.

6 Continue shaping the biscuits, transferring them to a wire rack as they cool and crisp. If the biscuits become too crisp to shape, return the baking sheet to the hot oven for 15–30 seconds to soften them, then continue as before.

VARIATION: A few chopped glacé fruits could be sprinkled over the top of the biscuits with the almonds, if liked.

Chocolate Marzipan Cookies

These crisp cookies – with a little almond surprise inside – are perfect for those with a sweet tooth.

Makes about 36

INGREDIENTS
200 g/7 oz/scant 1 cup unsalted butter, softened, plus extra for greasing
200 g/7 oz/scant 1 cup light muscovado sugar
1 egg
300 g/11 oz/2⅔ cups plain flour, plus extra for dusting
60 ml/4 tbsp cocoa powder
200 g/7 oz white marzipan
115 g/4 oz white chocolate, broken into squares

3 Roll out about half the dough on a lightly floured surface to about 5 mm/¼ in thick. Using a 5 cm/2 in biscuit cutter, cut out rounds, re-rolling the dough as required until you have about 36 rounds.

1 Preheat the oven to 190°C/375°F/Gas 5. Lightly grease two large baking sheets. Cream the butter with the sugar in a bowl until pale and fluffy. Add the egg and beat well.

2 Sift the flour and cocoa over the mixture. Stir in, first with a wooden spoon, then with clean hands, pressing the mixture together to make a fairly soft dough.

4 Cut the marzipan into about 36 equal pieces. Roll into balls, flatten slightly and place one on each round of dough. Roll out the remaining dough, cut out more rounds, then place on top of the almond paste. Press the dough edges to seal.

5 Bake for 10–12 minutes, or until the cookies have risen well and are beginning to crack on the surface. Leave on the baking sheet to cool slightly for about 2–3 minutes, then transfer to a wire rack to cool completely.

6 Melt the white chocolate, then either drizzle it over the biscuits to decorate or spoon into a paper piping bag and quickly pipe a design on them.

COOK'S TIP: If the dough is too sticky to roll, chill it for about 30 minutes, then try again.

Ladies' Kisses

These old-fashioned Italian cookies make pretty petits fours for a dinner party.

Makes 20

INGREDIENTS
150 g/5 oz/10 tbsp butter, softened
115 g/4 oz/generous ½ cup caster sugar
1 egg yolk
2.5 ml/½ tsp almond essence
115 g/4 oz/1 cup ground almonds
175 g/6 oz/1½ cups plain flour
50 g/2 oz plain chocolate

1 Cream the butter and sugar together with an electric mixer until light and fluffy, then beat in the yolk, almond essence, almonds and flour until evenly mixed. Chill until firm.

2 Preheat the oven to 160°C/325°F/ Gas 3. Line three to four baking sheets with non-stick baking paper. Break off small pieces of dough and roll into 40 balls. Place well apart on the baking sheets.

3 Bake for 20 minutes, or until golden. Remove the baking sheets from the oven, lift off the paper with the biscuits on, then place on wire racks to cool.

4 Lift the cold biscuits off the paper. Melt the chocolate and use it to sandwich the biscuits in pairs. Leave to cool and set before serving.

Tea Biscuits

If you don't want to pipe the mixture, spoon it on to the baking sheets and press with a fork.

Makes 20

INGREDIENTS
150 g/5 oz/10 tbsp butter, softened
75 g/3 oz/¾ cup icing sugar, sifted
1 egg, beaten
a few drops of almond essence
225 g/8 oz/2 cups plain flour
2–3 large pieces of
    candied peel

1 Preheat the oven to 230°C/450°F/ Gas 8. Line two baking sheets with non-stick baking paper. Cream the butter and sugar with an electric mixer until light and fluffy, then beat in the egg, almond essence and flour until evenly mixed.

2 Spoon the mixture into a piping bag fitted with a star nozzle and pipe 10 rosette shapes on each of the baking sheets.

3 Cut the candied peel into small diamond shapes and press one diamond into the centre of each biscuit. Bake for 5 minutes, or until golden. Transfer the biscuits on the baking sheet to a wire rack to cool completely. Lift the biscuits off the paper when cool.

Right: Ladies' Kisses (top); Tea Biscuits

Mocha Viennese Swirls

Some temptations just can't be resisted. Put out a plate of these melt-in-the-mouth marvels and watch them vanish.

Makes about 20

INGREDIENTS
200 g/7 oz/scant 1 cup unsalted butter,
    softened, plus extra for greasing
115 g/4 oz plain chocolate, broken
    into squares
50 g/2 oz/½ cup icing sugar
30 ml/2 tbsp strong black coffee
200 g/7 oz/scant 2 cups plain flour
50 g/2 oz/½ cup cornflour

FOR THE DECORATION
about 20 blanched almonds
150 g/5 oz plain chocolate

2 Spoon the mixture into a piping bag fitted with a large star nozzle and pipe about 20 swirls on the baking sheets, allowing room for spreading during baking.

3 Press an almond into the centre of each swirl. Bake for about 15 minutes, or until the biscuits are firm and just beginning to brown. Leave to cool for about 10 minutes on the baking sheets, then transfer to a wire rack to cool completely.

1 Preheat the oven to 190°C/375°F/Gas 5. Lightly grease two large baking sheets. Melt the plain chocolate in a bowl over hot water. Cream the butter with the icing sugar in a bowl until smooth and pale. Beat in the melted chocolate, then the coffee. Sift the plain flour and cornflour over the mixture. Fold in lightly and evenly to make a soft mixture.

4 When cold, melt the plain chocolate for the decoration, and dip the base of each swirl to coat. Place the coated biscuits on a sheet of non-stick baking paper and leave to set.

COOK'S TIP: If the mixture is too stiff to pipe, soften it with a little more black coffee.

Fudgy Glazed Chocolate Bars

For a simpler bar, omit the fudge glaze and dust with icing sugar instead.

Serves 8–10

INGREDIENTS

115 g/4 oz/½ cup unsalted butter, cut into
 pieces, plus extra for greasing
250 g/9 oz bittersweet or semi-sweet
 chocolate, chopped
25 g/1 oz unsweetened chocolate, chopped
90 g/3½ oz/scant ½ cup light brown sugar
50 g/2 oz/¼ cup granulated sugar
2 eggs
15 ml/1 tbsp vanilla essence
65 g/2½ oz/9 tbsp plain flour
115 g/4 oz/⅔ cup pecan nuts or walnuts,
 toasted and chopped
150 g/5 oz fine quality white chocolate,
 chopped into 5 mm/¼ in pieces
pecan halves to decorate (optional)

FUDGY CHOCOLATE GLAZE
175 g/6 oz semi-sweet or bittersweet
 chocolate, chopped
50 g/2 oz/¼ cup unsalted butter, cut into pieces
30 ml/2 tbsp corn or golden syrup
10 ml/2 tsp vanilla essence
5 ml/1 tsp instant coffee powder

1 Preheat the oven to 180°C/350°F/
Gas 4. Invert a 20 cm/8 in square cake
tin and mould a piece of foil over it.
Turn it over and line with the
moulded foil. Lightly grease the foil.

2 In a medium saucepan over a low
heat, melt the dark chocolates and
butter until smooth, stirring frequently.

3 Remove the pan from heat. Stir in
the sugars and continue stirring for
2 more minutes, until they dissolve.
Beat in the eggs and vanilla and stir in
the flour until just blended. Stir in the
pecan nuts or walnuts and white
chocolate. Pour the batter into the
prepared tin.

4 Bake for 20–25 minutes, or until a
cocktail stick inserted 5 cm/2 in from
the centre comes out with just a few
crumbs attached (do not overbake or
the "cake" will be dry). Remove the
tin to a wire rack to cool for about
30 minutes. Using the foil to lift,
remove the "cake" from the tin and
cool on the rack for at least 2 hours.

5 Prepare the glaze. In a medium saucepan over a medium heat, melt the chocolate, butter, syrup, vanilla essence and coffee powder, stirring frequently, until smooth. Remove from the heat. Chill for 1 hour, or until thickened and spreadable.

6 Invert the "cake" on to the wire rack and remove the foil. Turn top-side up. Using a metal palette knife, spread a thick layer of fudgy glaze over the top. Chill for 1 hour, until set. Cut into bars. If you wish, top each with a pecan half.

Glazed Gingerbread Biscuits

The quantity of these little biscuits that you can make depends on the size of the cutters you use.

Makes about 20

INGREDIENTS
175 g/6 oz/1½ cups plain flour, plus extra
    for dusting
1.5 ml/¼ tsp bicarbonate of soda
5 ml/1 tsp ground ginger
5 ml/1 tsp ground cinnamon
65 g/2½ oz/5 tbsp unsalted butter, cut into
    pieces, plus extra for greasing
75 g/3 oz/scant ½ cup caster sugar
30 ml/2 tbsp maple or golden syrup
1 egg yolk, beaten
red and green food colouring
175 g/6 oz white marzipan
salt

ICING GLAZE
30 ml/2 tbsp lightly beaten egg white
30 ml/2 tbsp lemon juice
175–225 g/6–8 oz/1½–2 cups icing sugar

1 Sift together the flour, bicarbonate of soda, spices and a pinch of salt into a large bowl. Rub in the butter until the mixture resembles fine breadcrumbs. Add the sugar, syrup and egg yolk and mix to a firm dough. Knead lightly, wrap and chill for 30 minutes.

2 Preheat the oven to 180°C/350°F/ Gas 4. Grease a large baking sheet. Roll out the dough on a floured surface and stamp out decorative shapes with novelty biscuit cutters.

3 Transfer to the prepared sheet and bake for 8–10 minutes, until the biscuits are beginning to colour around the edges. Leave on the baking sheet for 2 minutes, then transfer to a wire rack to cool.

4 To make the glaze, mix the egg white and lemon juice in a bowl. Gradually beat in the icing sugar until the mixture is smooth and has the consistency of thin cream. Place the wire rack over a tray or plate. Spoon the icing glaze over the biscuits until they are completely covered. Leave in a cool place to dry for several hours.

5 Knead red food colouring into half the marzipan and green into the other half. Roll a thin length of each piece and then twist together into a rope. Secure a rope of marzipan around a biscuit, dampening the icing with a little water, if necessary, to hold the marzipan twist in place. Repeat on about half the biscuits.

6 Dilute a little of each food colouring with water. Using a fine brush, paint decorations on the plain biscuits. Leave to dry.

COOK'S TIP: These biscuits can be made to suit the occasion, such as Christmas, as here, or birthdays.

Christmas Biscuits

These festive biscuits would make a lovely present – as well as a special teatime treat on Christmas day.

Makes about 12

INGREDIENTS
75 g/3 oz/6 tbsp butter, plus extra
    for greasing
50 g/2 oz/½ cup icing sugar
finely grated rind of 1 small lemon
1 egg yolk
175 g/6 oz/1½ cups plain flour, plus extra
    for dusting
salt

TO DECORATE
2 egg yolks
red and green food colouring

1 In a large bowl, beat the butter, sugar and lemon rind together until pale and fluffy. Beat in the egg yolk, and then sift in the flour and a pinch of salt. Knead together to form a smooth dough. Wrap in clear film and chill for 30 minutes.

2 Preheat the oven to190°C/375°F/ Gas 5. Lightly grease two baking sheets. On a lightly floured surface, roll out the dough to 3 mm/⅛ in thick.

3 Using a 6 cm/2½ in fluted cutter, stamp out as many biscuits as you can, with the cutter dipped in flour to prevent it from sticking to the dough. Transfer the biscuits to the prepared sheets.

4 For the decoration, mark the biscuits lightly with a 2.5 cm/1 in holly leaf cutter and use a 5 mm/¼ in plain piping nozzle for the berries. Chill for 10 minutes, until firm.

5 Put each egg yolk for the decoration into a small cup. Mix red food colouring into one and green food colouring into the other. Using a small brush, paint the colours on to the biscuits. Bake for 10–12 minutes, or until they begin to colour around the edges. Cool slightly on the baking sheets, then transfer to a wire rack.

Hogmanay Shortbread

Light, crisp shortbread looks so professional when shaped in a mould, although you could also shape it by hand.

**Makes 2 large or
8 individual shortbreads**

INGREDIENTS
175 g/6 oz/1½ cups plain flour, plus extra
    for dusting
50 g/2 oz/½ cup cornflour
50 g/2 oz/¼ cup caster sugar, plus extra
    for sprinkling
115 g/4 oz/½ cup unsalted butter, cut into
    small pieces

1 Preheat the oven to 160°C/325°F/ Gas 3. Lightly flour the mould and line a baking sheet with non-stick baking paper. Sift the flour, cornflour and sugar into a mixing bowl. Rub the butter into the flour mixture until it binds together and you can knead it into a soft dough.

COOK'S TIP: Wrap in cellophane paper and decorate with a tartan ribbon to make a delicious home-made gift.

2 Place half the dough into the mould and press to fit neatly. Invert the mould on to the baking sheet and tap firmly to release the dough shape. Repeat. If not using a mould, place the shortbread mixture in two mounds on the baking sheet and press into 13 cm/ 5 in rounds. Use a knife to mark four portions, if liked.

3 Bake for 35–40 minutes, or 15–20 minutes for individual shortbreads, until pale golden.

4 Sprinkle the top of the shortbread with a little caster sugar and cool on the baking sheet.

Coffee Sponge Drops

Low fat cheese and stem ginger make a delicious filling for these lovely
light sponge drops.

Makes 12

INGREDIENTS
50 g/2 oz/½ cup plain flour
15 ml/1 tbsp instant coffee powder
2 eggs
75 g/3 oz/scant ½ cup caster sugar

FOR THE FILLING
115 g/4 oz/¼ cup low-fat soft cheese
40 g/1½ oz/¼ cup chopped
   stem ginger

2 Combine the eggs and caster sugar
in a bowl. Beat with a hand-held
electric whisk until thick and mousse-
like (when the whisk is lifted a trail
should remain on the surface of the
mixture for at least 15 seconds).

1 Preheat the oven to 190°C/375°F/
Gas 5. Line two baking sheets with
non-stick baking paper. Make the
filling by beating together the soft
cheese and stem ginger. Chill until
required. Sift the flour and instant
coffee powder together.

VARIATION: If liked, use the zest
of one orange in place of the stem
ginger and add 15 ml/1 tbsp
caster sugar.

3 Carefully add the sifted flour and
coffee mixture and gently fold in with
a metal spoon.

4 Spoon the mixture into a piping
bag fitted with a 1 cm/½ in plain
nozzle. Pipe 4 cm/1½ in rounds on the
baking sheets. Bake for 12 minutes.
Cool on a wire rack. Sandwich
together with the filling.

Oaty Crisps

Made with polyunsaturated sunflower oil, these crunchy biscuits make a healthy snack. Ideal with morning coffee or to add to childrens' lunch boxes for the mid-morning break or with lunch.

Makes 18

INGREDIENTS
60 ml/4 tbsp sunflower oil, plus extra
    for brushing
175 g/6 oz/1¾ cups rolled oats
75 g/3 oz/scant ½ cup light
    muscovado sugar
1 egg
30 ml/2 tbsp malt extract

1 Preheat the oven to 190°C/375°F/ Gas 5. Lightly brush two baking sheets with sunflower oil. Mix the rolled oats and muscovado sugar in a bowl, breaking up any lumps in the sugar. Add the egg, sunflower oil and malt extract, mix well, then leave to soak for 15 minutes.

VARIATION: To give these crisp biscuits a coarser texture, substitute jumbo oats for some or all of the rolled oats.

2 Using a teaspoon, place small heaps of the mixture well apart on the prepared baking sheets. Press the heaps into 7.5 cm/3 in rounds with the back of a dampened fork.

3 Bake the biscuits for 10–15 minutes, or until golden brown. Leave them on the baking sheet to cool slightly for 1 minute, then transfer to a wire rack to cool completely.

COOK'S TIP: These biscuits will keep for up to a week in an airtight container.

Apricot Yogurt Cookies

You can afford to indulge yourself with these low-fat, low-cholesterol, flavour-packed fruity cookies.

Makes 16

INGREDIENTS
45 ml/3 tbsp sunflower oil, plus extra
    for brushing
175 g/6 oz/1½ cups plain flour
5 ml/1 tsp baking powder
5 ml/1 tsp ground cinnamon
75 g/3 oz/scant 1 cup rolled oats
75 g/3 oz/scant ½ cup light
    muscovado sugar
115 g/4 oz/½ cup chopped ready-to-eat
    dried apricots
15 ml/1 tbsp flaked almonds or
    chopped hazelnuts
150 ml/¼ pint/⅔ cup natural yogurt
demerara sugar,
    for sprinkling

2 Beat together the yogurt and oil, then stir evenly into the mixture to make a firm dough. If necessary, add a little more yogurt.

3 Use your hands to roll the mixture into about 16 small balls, place on the baking sheet and flatten with a fork. Sprinkle with demerara sugar.

1 Preheat the oven to 190°C/375°F/ Gas 5. Lightly oil a large baking sheet. Stir together the flour, baking powder and cinnamon. Stir in the oats, sugar, apricots and nuts.

VARIATIONS: If liked, use unsulphured dried apricots, as these have a richer flavour. Dried dates could replace the apricots.

4 Bake for 15–20 minutes, or until firm and golden brown. Transfer to a wire rack to cool.

COOK'S TIP: These cookies do not keep well, so it is best to eat them within two days, or to freeze them. Pack into a polythene bag and freeze for up to four months.

Low in fat and sugar, high in
crunch factor and flavour – what
better for a picnic?

Makes 16

INGREDIENTS
oil, for brushing
115 g/4 oz/½ cup low-fat spread
60 ml/4 tbsp rice syrup
50 g/2 oz/½ cup wholemeal flour
225 g/8 oz/generous 2 cups
    rolled oats
50 g/2 oz/⅓ cup pine nuts

1 Preheat the oven to 180°C/350°F/
Gas 4. Line a 20 cm/8 in shallow
baking tin with oiled foil. Melt the
low-fat spread and rice syrup in a
small saucepan over a low heat, then
stir in the flour, oats and pine nuts
until well mixed.

2 Tip the mixture into the tin and
pat it out evenly with your fingers.
Press the mixture down lightly. Bake
for 25–30 minutes, until the flapjacks
are lightly browned and crisp. Mark
into squares while still warm. Cool
slightly, then transfer to a wire rack.

COOK'S TIP: Do not let the syrup
mixture boil or the flapjacks will be
tacky rather than crisp.

Right: Flapjacks (top); Ginger Figures

Ginger Figures

Surprisingly, each of these
charming, plump little figures
contains less than 2 grams of fat.

Makes 8

INGREDIENTS
115 g/4 oz/1 cup plain flour, sifted,
    plus extra for dusting
7.5 ml/1½ tsp ground ginger
grated rind of 1 orange and 1 lemon
75 ml/5 tbsp pear and apple spread
25 g/1 oz/ 2 tbsp low-fat spread
16 currants and 8 raisins, to decorate

1 Preheat the oven to 180°C/350°F/
Gas 4. Mix the flour, ginger and grated
orange and lemon rind in a bowl. Melt
the pear and apple spread and the low-
fat spread in a small saucepan over a
low heat.

2 As soon as the pear and apple spread
mixture has melted, stir it into the dry
ingredients. Mix to a firm dough in the
bowl, then remove the dough, wrap it
in clear film and chill for 2–3 hours.

3 Roll out the dough on a lightly
floured surface to a thickness of about
5 mm/¼ in. Cut out gingerbread men,
using a cutter or a template.

4 Use currants for eyes and raisins for
noses. Draw a mouth using the point
of a knife. Place the biscuits on a
lightly floured baking sheet and bake
for 8–10 minutes. Cool on a wire rack.

Fresh Orange Cookies

These moreish little cookies demonstrate perfectly that you do not have to sacrifice flavour to cut down fat.

Makes 30

INGREDIENTS

115 g/4 oz/½ cup low-fat spread, plus
   extra for greasing
200 g/7 oz/1 cup
   caster sugar
2 egg yolks
15 ml/1 tbsp fresh orange juice
grated rind of 1 orange
165 g/6 oz/1½ cups plain flour
2.5 ml/½ tsp salt
5 ml/1 tsp baking powder

1 With an electric mixer, cream the low-fat spread and sugar until light and fluffy. Add the yolks, orange juice and rind, and continue beating to blend. Set aside.

> VARIATION: The orange juice and rind could be replaced with lemon for a change.

2 In another bowl, sift together the flour, salt and baking powder. Add to the orange mixture and stir until it forms a dough. Wrap the dough in greaseproof paper and chill for 2 hours.

3 Preheat the oven to 190°C/375°F/ Gas 5. Grease two baking sheets. Roll spoonfuls of the dough into balls and place 2.5–5 cm/1–2 in apart on the prepared sheets.

4 Press down with a fork to flatten slightly. Bake the cookies for 8–10 minutes, or until golden brown. Transfer to a wire rack to cool.

Southwater is an imprint of
Anness Publishing Ltd
Hermes House
88–89 Blackfriars Road,
London SE1 8HA
tel. 020 7401 2077
fax 020 7633 9499

Distributed in the USA by
Anness Publishing Inc.
27 West 20th Street
Suite 504, New York NY 10011
tel. 212 807 6739
fax 212 807 6813

Distributed in the UK by
The Manning Partnership
251–253 London Road East
Batheaston
Bath BA1 7RL
tel. 01225 852 727
fax 01225 852 852

Distributed in Australia by
Sandstone Publishing
Unit 1, 360 Norton Street, Leichhardt
New South Wales 2040
tel. 02 9560 7888
fax 02 9560 7488

© 2000 Anness Publishing Limited

1 3 5 7 9 10 8 6 4 2

Publisher: Joanna Lorenz
Editor: Valerie Ferguson
Series Designer: Bobbie Colgate Stone
Designer: Andrew Heath
Production Controller: Joanna King

Recipes contributed by: Catherine Atkinson,
Alex Barker, Michelle Berriedale-Johnson,
Angela Boggiano, Kathy Brown, Carla Capalbo,
Frances Cleary, Carole Clements, Trish Davies,
Joanna Farrow, Christine France, Carole Handslip,
Rebekah Hassan, Lesley Mackley, Norma Miller,
Sallie Morris, Janice Murfitt, Anne Sheasby,
Liz Trigg, Elizabeth Wolf-Cohen, Jeni Wright.

Photography: William Adams-Lingwood,
Karl Adamson, Edward Allwright, Steve Baxter,
James Duncan, Ian Garlick, Michelle Garrett,
Amanda Heywood, Janine Hosegood,
David Jordan, Debbie Patterson.

Notes:
For all recipes, quantities are given in both metric
and imperial measures and, where appropriate,
measures are also given in standard cups
and spoons.
Follow one set, but not a mixture, because they
are not interchangeable.

Standard spoon and cup measures are level.

1 tsp = 5 ml   1 tbsp = 15 ml

1 cup = 250 ml/8 fl oz

Australian standard tablespoons are 20 ml.
Australian readers should use 3 tsp in place of
1 tbsp for measuring small quantities of gelatine,
cornflour, salt etc.

Medium eggs are used unless otherwise stated.

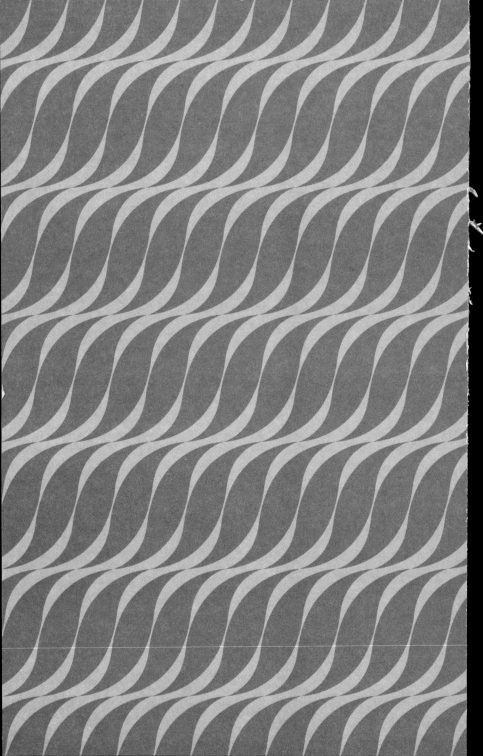